The Money Tree

The Money Tree

The Roots & Fruits of Poverty & Prosperity

Garrett B. Gunderson

MEDIA

Published 2019 by Gildan Media LLC
aka G&D Media
www.GandDmedia.com

Front Cover design by David Rheinhardt of Pyrographx

Interior design by Meghan Day Healey of Story Horse, LLC

Library of Congress Cataloging-in-Publication Data is available upon request

ISBN: 978-1-7225-0122-8

10   9   8   7   6   5   4   3   2   1

THIS BOOK IS DEDICATED TO THE TRUE
PRODUCERS WHO HAVE INTERNALIZED AND
HUMBLY LIVED THE PRINCIPLES OF PROSPERITY
IN THE FACE OF SCARCITY AND CHALLENGES.

Contents

Introduction

The Greater Purpose

Imagine that you were faced with the most critical decision of your life. If you had access to a crystal ball and could see the natural results of that decision, how would that affect your decision? Would it be much easier to choose correctly?

The purpose of this book is to show how abundance is achieved through awareness. Many people don't even realize when they are in scarcity and therefore remain stuck. This book will outline how to recognize scarcity and then choose abundance while detailing the natural results of our choices. The more people are aware of the results of their choices, the better, more informed decisions they can make. My hope is that by showing you what happens to individuals and societies who choose either scarcity or abundance, you can make a conscious choice long before you ever experience those results for yourself. In other words, this book is the crystal ball of your personal prosperity.

In contrast to most books you will read on the subject of personal finance, I should inform you up front that this is not a "feel-good" book that will get you excited about getting rich without giving you real substance, nor is it a product and strategy-centered book that will give you hot stock tips or debt reduction strategies without providing proper background.

The purpose of this book is to provide an in-depth framework that helps people to see the entire process of wealth creation, from start to finish. It is to explain the direct relationship between both philosophy and strategy, between paradigms and results. In other words, this book plainly and unflinchingly provides the context that all other money books fit into;in other words, you can make sense of or judge the value of any other financial book using this book as the standard. With an increased awareness you can discern truth from falsehood in your personal financial life. While most financial books are about either philosophy or application, this is a book about the context in which both philosophies and strategies exist. Greater context leads to deeper understanding, which in turn leads to better results.

Although my main focus is on context, I also want to ensure that my readers are left with a clear direction of where they can go after reading the book. There's absolutely no way that I could ever explain everything I know about money and prosperity in such a short book, which is why I have developed many other tools and educational resources to help you live your ideal life. The best way for most people to begin applying what they learn here is through the Producer Power Hour Mastermind (ProducerPowerHour.com), which is outlined in detail in chapter seven.

Throughout this book, I will show you how the source, or root, of prosperity is actually you, not a breakthrough product or a cutting edge technique. It will train you to trace your results back to their origins, so that you can fundamentally transform the way you view wealth and your role in its creation. This book focuses on the philosophies, paradigms and principles underlying all human action in order to help you see through traditional hype and marketing of the financial industry, choose the correct strategies which best align with your unique gifts, and get the results that reflect your true nature as a being of immense value creation.

If you're reading this book because you're looking for a quick-fix or a way to get rich quick, stop reading now; you simply will not find that here. On the other hand, this book is perfect for you if any of the following is true:

- *You're looking for deeper answers and more viable solutions to your money issues than you've found in most media sources*
- *You're willing to question the status quo*
- *You're seeking to learn and understand the fundamental principles governing financial strategies and results*

- *You're looking for appropriate methodologies and strategies that actually work and give you powerful results*
- *You feel a sense of mission in your life, and you must prosper in order to fulfill your personal mission*
- *You want to learn how to prosper consistently and sustainably, regardless of external circumstance, including and especially financial markets*
- *You want to learn how money can flow through you, where you are the figurative money tree*

This is not a book about the stock market; it's a book about contribution, about human greatness, and about true prosperity beyond money. It's a book for people who see greater purpose in being wealthy than personal comfort, status, and prestige. Furthermore, this book will help you to get rid of scarcity in your life through increased awareness and ways to overcome the destructive mode of scarcity and ultimately to cultivate a paradigm of abundance.

Most financial teachings today originate from a paradigm of scarcity. With such a root, it's no wonder that the fruits of such teachings are limited at best and destructive at worst. No matter how good the intention, the advice and action based primarily on the scarcity paradigm can never lead to the results that we all want financially.

Keep reading as I uncover the truth about retirement planning, outline the proper philosophies and principles that true wealth is based on, and help you to practically apply those fundamentals utilizing appropriate products and strategies.

Also, take a moment to familiarize yourself with the following model of prosperity, which I call The Money Tree, before you continue reading, as this will be referred to throughout the book.

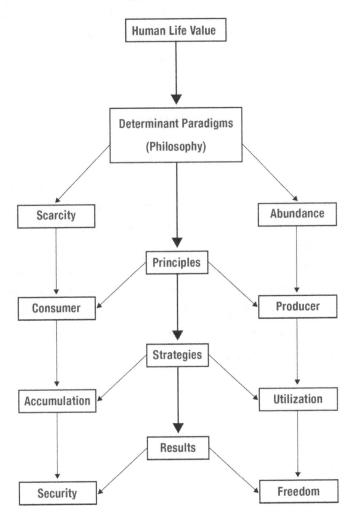

In order to secure and implement your greatest results, I have created a mastermind group that is designed to help you accomplish your objectives. Regardless of your background or current situation, this is designed to make a lasting and profound change in your life.

For lasting and profound transformation in your life there are four essentials:

1. Education (access to new information and tools)
2. Mentoring (sounding board, tailored guidance, leadership)
3. Association (like-minded individuals)
4. Accountability (support and structure to facilitate results)

I am covering number 1 in this book.

To access number 2, 3, & 4 there is an opportunity to join the Producer Power Hour Mastermind. These 4 components of success are essential in having sustainable results. I have such a passion for implementation and lasting results that I want you to try the Mastermind for FREE.

My life's mission is to have 1 million people reach financial independence and I would love for you to be one of them. Go to ProducerPowerHour.com to take the next step in your journey to sustainable wealth and living abundantly.

Chapter 1

From Planting to Harvesting

A parable of gardeners and trees outlined. Each element of the parable represents ingredients that determine either poverty or prosperity results.

"It was planted in a good soil by great waters, that it might bring forth branches, and that it might bear fruit, that it might be a goodly vine . . . being planted, shall it prosper?"
—EZEKIEL 17:8 & 10

Let me begin with a parable. Two gardeners planted fruit trees in their gardens. The first gardener took care to select the best seeds. Furthermore, he carefully prepared the soil, picking the ideal location that would receive adequate water and sunlight, tilling it well, and providing fertilizer.

From those seeds sprung forth healthy, strong, and deep roots that gave the trees life and good health. The tree trunks grew straight and strong, and gave them the ability to withstand the strongest of winds. Healthy branches grew from the trees, profuse and strong enough to hold plentiful fruit. After a time, the trees produced the best, biggest, and most delicious fruit that the farmer had ever seen and tasted. It was the best harvest he had, and many came from miles around to buy his fruit and enjoy his harvest.

The second gardener, on the other hand, was careless about his selection of both his seeds and his soil. The soil he planted in was rocky and hard, had few nutrients, and was a poor location for water and sunlight. Most of his seeds never germinated and took root. The few that did had shallow, unhealthy roots. From those roots grew narrow, twisted, and flimsy trunks that were nonresistant to the elements. The branches were few and weak, and the trees produced wormy, small, and bitter fruit that nobody wanted.

How does this parable apply to your prosperity? Each of the images portrayed represent ingredients in the process of either a life of poverty or a life of prosperity.

The symbol of the gardener is you, or what I will call your human life value. Human life value is everything you are when all of your material resources are stripped away. It is your knowledge, your character and integrity, your ability to think creatively and uniquely, your relationships, your faith, your virtue—or the lack of each of these things. It is your knowledge and ability to shape materials and information in new ways that are valued and utilized by others and yourself. What do you bring to the world? What is your unique combination of talents, abilities, education and perspective? This is your human life value. You become productive and access your potential by utilizing your human life value in the service of others.

Insight

"I don't remember exactly how old I was, but there was a time in my childhood when I would ask my Dad for things and he would tell me, "We need to wait for the money tree to bloom." I believed him literally, and I remember sitting outside watching one tree in particular in our front yard, waiting for it to bloom. I would even check up on it periodically, thinking that as soon is it bloomed we would have money.

It's a funny story, but it also carries a lot of meaning. I was so ready to see money that I didn't even care what he said, and it led to unquestioned beliefs. I sat there waiting without taking proactive action.

So many people plant their "seeds" of prosperity in the wrong soil, they fail to cultivate and water them, then are disappointed when no money appears. They operate under faulty perceptions, which results in a failure to cultivate the right habits. They're waiting for something to happen or someone to help them, rather than taking immediate and practical action to improve their lives.

Your money tree can bloom, but only if it's planted correctly and cultivated carefully.

The seeds, soil, water, and sunlight represent your paradigm, or the way that you view the world that determines how you interact with the world and other people. Specifically, there are two determinant paradigms that people have to choose from: scarcity and abundance.

From the seeds of scarcity come roots of fear, doubt, and worry. From the seeds of abundance come roots of faith, hope, and love. The tree trunks represent principles: the timeless, unchanging, universal natural laws of the universe that, when applied appropriately, provide stability, strength and direction in a person's life.

The tree branches represent strategies, techniques, tools, and resources. The strategies I use and how I use them are determined by our human life value, our paradigm, and our understanding and application of principles. And finally, the fruits of the trees represent the results I experience from the combination of my human life value, my paradigm, principles, and strategies.

Consider the following chart for a moment:

	Abundant Seed	Scarce Seed
Abundant Soil	Productive Growth	Death No-Growth
Scarce Soil	Death No-Growth	Destructive Growth

PROSPERITY

Abundance

Scarcity

POVERTY

I've learned that the starting place to grow your money trees is with your soil and your seeds. Seeds are the principles that you're aligned with and the soil is who you currently are.

Note quadrant III: If you attempt to plant a seed of abundance in scarce soil, the result will be no growth and death of the seed. Why? Because when you're in scarcity you will reject seeds of abundance, they cannot take root because you are not the kind of soil conducive to prosperous growth.

Similarly, if you have abundant soil, or in other words, if you are full of hope, faith, love, and abundance, but you then plant a seed of scarcity, whether through friends, family, the media, or society, your soil will reject that seed and it cannot grow (Quadrant II).

In quadrant IV we find both scarce soil and scarce seeds—resulting, of course, in scarcity and poverty in every area of one's life.

On the other hand, in quadrant I we find ourselves in a position where our soil is abundant, and the seeds (or principles) planted within that soil are abundant, we will experience favorable conditions for productive growth and the seed will grow.

Remember: You have the power to control and change your soil, and to nurture and cultivate it. In the end I have the power and the control to change my soil, to nurture it and to cultivate it.

This parable describes a model that I have created called The Money Tree. The Money Tree looks like the illustration on the following page:

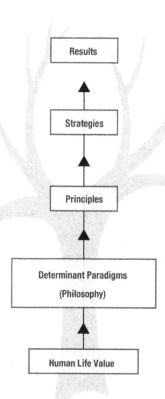

Chapter 2

The Necessary Elements

Both theory and application are necessary for financial success. Prosperity is a predictable formula: Human Life Value + Sound Philosophy + Correct Principles + Wise Application = Results. Soul Purpose elevates our motivation to prosper and to realize our full potential. Two paradigms, scarcity and abundance, determine the quality and longevity of financial results.

In order for a tree to grow and flourish, it begins with the proper soil. The next elements are a seed, then roots, a trunk, branches, and leaves, all of which determine the fruit. Prosperity also requires that every necessary element in the process be present.

Have you ever read a book about personal finance that got you excited about the idea, or the philosophy of prosperity, and then left you hanging wondering, "Okay, now what do I do?" Or, have you read other books that tried to convince you to buy into specific products and strategies without explaining the prin-

ciples behind them, leaving you skeptical and unfulfilled? It seems that too often people are either left
without clear direction on how to practically apply
theory, or pressured into buying products without
understanding their relevance or context in our life.

But what if you could have the best of both worlds?
What would happen in your financial life if you understood the correct philosophies, paradigms and principles governing prosperity and you had the knowledge
and ability to practically apply them, using products
and strategies?

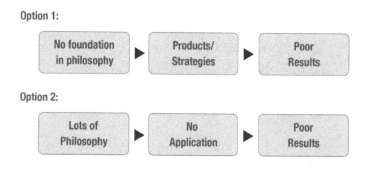

Prosperity is a predictable formula: proper philosophies + paradigms + correct principles + products/
strategies = results. A person who understands sound
financial philosophies and principles but who does not
practically apply them is impotent and ineffectual. On
the other hand, a person who bases their entire financial plan on products and techniques, without understanding the underlying philosophies and principles,
is ungrounded, limited, and in many cases, actually
destructive. In other words, it's essential that both the-

ory and application be present for a person to achieve true financial success.

Also, it's critically important to realize that who you are as an individual is far more important than any other ingredient in the recipe of prosperity. The utilization of your human life value is the single biggest determinant of your financial success, or lack thereof. It is through your human life value that you are even able to comprehend philosophy and everything that follows.

Any time anyone asks me what I think they should invest in, my answer is always the same: "Invest in yourself until you know and even when you know, never stop investing in yourself." Once a person's Human Life Value gets to a certain point through discipline, education, and practice, they have no need to ask such a question. Human Life Value is always, without exception, the best and most important place to start the pursuit of prosperity.

Option 3:

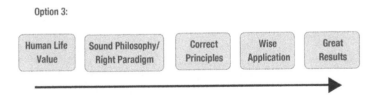

Throughout this book, I'm going to be comparing prosperity to growing a tree: Human life value is the gardener that plants the tree; philosophy and paradigms are the seeds, soil, and water; either fear, doubt, and worry, or faith, hope, and love are the roots; principles are the trunk; and financial products and strategies are the branches and leaves. The fruits of our prosperity tree are the natural results of everything that comes before them.

Most of the financial advice you read and hear comes from one of two camps: those who talk about nothing but the root and trunk of prosperity, or those who talk about nothing but the branches and leaves. These views are not so much wrong as they are incomplete. My purpose is to bridge the gap between these two camps and provide a more holistic view of finances that is simultaneously idealistic and practical.

Having said this, however, it must be stressed that, although these two views are equally important, there is a definite order in which they must be applied.

The Money Tree™

Here is the model of prosperity that we have built so far:

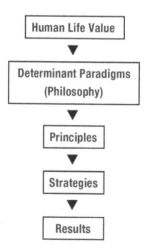

This model will be developed throughout the book, but this basic structure is the most important thing to grasp for now.

Soul Purpose™: The "Why" of Prosperity

The above model is useful to a person who is committed to creating financial prosperity. Why should a person want to prosper? What is the appropriate motivation to achieve wealth?

You have a mission to perform that no other individual can perform. When you do what you were born to do, you relieve a degree of pain or suffering in the world and invite more happiness in your own life. Ultimately, that's what prosperity economics is all about; finding and meeting human desires through service, solving problems and creating value. The more willing and able you are to serve others, the more value is returned to you, and the more you will prosper.

The mission I speak of is what I call Soul Purpose. Soul Purpose is comprised of your unique combination of ability, passion and values. Your Soul Purpose gives you unique perspectives, insight, and talents. When these are combined with purpose and applied productively and effectively, any individual can make an impact upon the world, their own family, and bring the highest levels of joy and fulfillment for themselves.

For an individual to fully realize Soul Purpose, prosperity is key. Prosperity means that they have access to every resource, material and otherwise, required to deliver value. Before ever investing in a product, it is critical to start out with the correct fundamental philosophies and principles, then investing only in financial products they truly understand.

Scarcity versus Abundance

The Money Tree is easy enough to grasp. However, even if a person were to follow the formula above (Human Life Value + Philosophy + Principles + Application = Results), what would happen throughout the process if the person's worldview and philosophies were incorrect and tainted? How would that influence the rest of his or her decisions? In other words, it's not enough to use philosophy; you must be operating under the correct philosophy.

The depth of the Money Tree model is unveiled when we understand that there are two basic philosophies, or determinant paradigms, that human beings have to choose from: scarcity and abundance.

The following chapters will detail each of these five steps of our Money Tree model of prosperity. Furthermore, they will detail the differences between a philosophy based on scarcity and a philosophy based on abundance, and the natural results that flow from each of these paradigms.

Chapter 3

Two Determinant Paradigms (Philosophy)

Human beings choose from two different paradigms, scarcity and abundance, which determine how they view and interact with the world. Scarcity leads to all destructive human tendencies; abundance induces all productive traits. Abundance is a choice.

"Two roads diverged in a wood, and I—I took the one less traveled by, and that has made all the difference."
—ROBERT FROST

Stephen R. Covey defined paradigms well when he wrote in *The 7 Habits of Highly Effective People*, "The word paradigm comes from the Greek. It was originally a scientific term, and is more commonly used today to mean a model, theory, perception, assumption, or frame of reference. In the more general sense, it's the way we 'see' the world—not in terms of our visual sense of sight, but in terms of perceiving, understanding, and interpreting."

Paradigms determine your actions, which determine your habits, which determine your results. The more healthy and aligned with truth your paradigm is, the better results you will experience.

When it comes to prosperity, there are two basic paradigms that you have to choose from: scarcity and abundance. These are what I call determinant paradigms, meaning that whichever one you are subject to determines how you view the world, how you treat others, how you react in any given situation, and what results you receive.

Contrast

It's a natural tendency among humans to view scarcity as bad and abundance as good. However, this is a simplistic view that ignores a fundamental truth about the nature of the universe, that being contrast.

Contrast is actually one of the greatest gifts ever given to us by God. Why? Because it is precisely through contrast that we have the power to choose. There is no choice except in the presence of opposites to choose from. Without contrast how could we appreciate happiness and joy if we have never experienced sadness and misery. In the absence of pain, there is less perspective for pleasure. It's through opposition, contrast and perspective that we find joy in achieving;

if everything were easy we would never feel fulfilled. It's through the contrast provided by opposition that we are able to learn and ultimately find context and meaning in existence.

Duality and contrast exists to give us the ability to choose from opposing thoughts and experiences. Your job is to identify and reject those things that bring ultimate suffering, and find and choose those things that bring ultimate happiness.

Discontentment and pain are gifts from a loving God that show you which of your actions are functional and right in the universe. They help you make course corrections by teaching you when you've made mistakes. They are like lighthouses guiding your way through the treacherous seas of choice.

Once again, it is through an awareness of scarcity that you are able to learn and can further understand and experience abundance. Scarcity and abundance, then, are presented to you as choices. Choosing scarcity leads to misery; choosing abundance leads to happiness.

Scarcity & Abundance

A scarcity paradigm is defined as the belief that resources are limited, and the world is a stage for a zero-sum game of accumulation. In a zero-sum game, anything that another wins is no longer available to all others playing the game. Further, these winnings are not replaced or transformed into anything of equivalent or greater value that remains in the game and is no therefore no longer available to other players. In the world of scarcity, ownership by another means the loss of opportunity for self. Scarcity-minded individuals seek to take from, exploit, and manipulate others to get what they want.

From intellectuals like Thomas Malthus, to capitalists who seek to destroy their competition, to individuals who desperately race to grab products off shelves before others get them, many people think and act as if there is a limited amount of material resources to share in the world, and limited ability to manipulate those resources for productive use.

Scarcity is characterized by the following conditions and perspectives:

Reasonable and Irrational   Myths

Fear, Doubt, and Worry   Ordinary

Blind Tradition & Skepticism

An abundance paradigm is the belief that possibilities are unlimited, and that the world offers everyone the ability to pursue and achieve their dreams. Abundance is characterized by happiness, joy, and love. Abundance-minded individuals do not feel a personal loss of resources when others have them. They seek to lift, serve, and bless the lives of others through their contribution.

Unreasonable and rational Faith, Confidence, and Peace	Self-assurance and Humility Healthy Critical Thinking Reality

Reasonable and irrational vs. unreasonable and rational

Scarcity appears to be reasonable because it's what's normal and customary in the world. Many things in life seem to support the fallacy of scarcity. For example, when people invest in real estate and end up losing money, most of them view this as a negative experience and "learn" that there is no money to be made in real estate. That experience is then ingrained into their psyche, and then influences every other decision they make; they begin to think that all investing is risky and that the only way to make money through investing is to get lucky. Scarcity appeals to our reason because it's normal for humans to find reasons why things will not work.

Although scarcity may appear to be reasonable, it's totally irrational. Scientifically and intuitively, we know that nature regenerates and with proper stewardship, has the ability to reproduce. Plants produce seeds, animals produce offspring, and human beings constantly create new ways to maximize and renew all of our sources of energy and food. Scarcity is not a reality; it is a deliberate illusion to provide opposition.

In a world dominated by a paradigm of scarcity, living abundantly seems unreasonable. So much negativity in the world supports scarcity and prevents us from seeing the abundance that surrounds us.

Abundance, however difficult to see, is completely rational. It is, in fact, the very nature of the universe. Water provides the conditions for existence for fish. However, fish do not see water because they were born into it and it's all they know. Abundance is similar to this in that it provides the conditions of our existence but may be difficult to see on a constant basis. Abundance is like the sun; it is always shining brightly even though clouds or the earth's rotation may temporarily block our view of it.

When most people in the world think, live, and act like scarcity is the nature of the universe, you must go against the grain and challenge traditional thinking in order to fully prosper.

Insight

When I was about to graduate college in the year 1999, I was receiving a lot of great job offers from many well-known companies. Most of my professors were advising me to take jobs simply because of the prestige, pay, benefits, and perceived security. It was the "reasonable" choice, but looking back on it, it would have been totally irrational.

I chose a different path and did what I loved to do and what was a better expression of my Soul Purpose. Those who were in scarcity thought, "How could you really do this on your own?" Fortunately, I talked with an abundant-minded Dean who said, "You're already doing great and you love what you do. Why would you go for some name or for some potential prestige for the university?" He understood that Soul Purpose is far more valuable than money or prestige.

That choice has changed my family's destiny. My life up to this point has mostly been spent in my Soul Purpose and has allowed me to keep expanding the expression of my Soul Purpose. This has provided me with inner peace and fulfillment that far outweighs any benefit I ever could have received by taking a route that may have initially looked more "secure."

I chose what at the time seemed to be unreasonable to many, which is precisely why I have been blessed with extraordinary results and have a life of joy and happiness.

Our mind can make up all kinds of "reasons" for doing or not doing anything. For example, I shouldn't enjoy the success that I have because I'm from a small town and a family of coal miners, I didn't come from money, etc. It takes looking beyond those reasons and taking a leap of faith to prosper. It takes moving forward when everything and everyone around you seem to be saying to stop trying. Prosperity is unreasonable because it transcends mental boundaries and falsely-perceived "reasons"

Fear, Doubt, & Worry vs.
Faith, Confidence, & Peace

The results are consistent and constantly plague us when we're gripped by scarcity: Fear, doubt, and worry. We fear that we will lose anything we have gained, we doubt that we have the ability to prosper or question if others will compensate us for our efforts, and we worry that there will never be enough money, food, time, etc.

Accepting abundance gives us faith in truth and principles, confidence that we can choose our destiny, and peace that everything we experience is for our good. While scarcity-minded people seem to fight and want to control life, abundance-minded people accept and live with harmony know that everything is perfect in the universe.

Jealousy & Pride vs.
Self-Assurance & Humility

Our fears lead us to compare ourselves to others; if we perceive others to be better than us in any way we put ourselves down and feel jealous, and if we perceive ourselves to be better than others we feel pride.

Through abundance we are able to recognize and therefore rid ourselves of jealousy and pride. In the absence of jealousy and pride, we enjoy self-assurance and humility. Envy dissolves and we stop comparing ourselves to others and live in alignment with our Soul

Purpose. We treat everyone with love; we relinquish any desire to have or take part in psychological hierarchies that bring so much conflict into the world.

Blind Tradition & Unhealthy Skepticism vs. Healthy critical Thinking

Blind tradition lives through fear and scarcity mode. We either follow the crowd blindly because we're too afraid to take independent action because of how we may look or what we think others may say or think about us. Or we may also be hoping to get lucky, or refuse to take much action at all because we're so afraid that others will take advantage of us.

> *"He who does anything because*
> *it is the custom, makes no choice."*
> —John Stuart Mill

Living abundantly does not mean that you become naïve, far from it. One must be careful of the counterfeit to abundance, which is ignorance. The truth is just the opposite: abundance helps you to be wise and do true due diligence without being negative, and to be open and excited about life without letting yourself get taken advantage of. Abundant investing is based on your Soul Purpose which is the most favorable condition for certainty and truth.

Myths vs. Reality

Scarcity aids us to fall prey to financial myths. These include such fallacies as: Investing is so difficult to understand you just have to turn it over to the experts, it takes money to make money, 401(k)s receive a 100% rate of return because of employer matches, and wealth is measured most effectively by net worth, just to name a few. These types of myths are made easy to buy into when we're looking to get something for nothing, when we're focused solely on price at the expense of cost and value, and when we're trying to cut expenses at all costs, all of which come from the scarcity paradigm.

"A long habit of not thinking a thing wrong, gives it a superficial appearance of being right, and raises at first a formidable outcry in defence of custom . . . Time makes more converts than reason."
—Thomas Paine

Through the lens of abundance you are able to see financial myths for what they are, and see the truth behind them. You are able to view everything through the proper context and judge things in the light of a macro perspective. This perspective is in alignment with our life and is consistent with our Soul Purpose. Through abundance we can analyze our financial decisions deeper and see how it can support our life today and money becomes a tool and resource to living Soul Purpose.

Ordinary vs. Extraordinary

Those subject to the scarcity paradigm live a life of limitations. Because their life is largely dictated by fear, rarely do they step outside of the ordinary. Many have ideas or ideals that are inside, but due to worry about what those on the outside will think or say, everything dies through doubt. Instead of expressing one's Soul Purpose, acceptance of the traditional dogma "go to school, get good grades, work at a stable corporation with good benefits, and retire at age 65" becomes the mantra.

By living abundantly, you access and develop your Soul Purpose to live a life of passion, service, contribution, and greatness. The greatest heroes and heroines in history are those who believed and acted like anything was possible. They had big goals and dreams and confidently and consistently pursued them despite any challenges or outside opinions propagating limitation.

"The most absurd and reckless aspirations have sometimes led to extraordinary success."
—Vauvenargues

Summary

In order to prosper, you must first start by developing your human life value. As your human life value increases, you become consciously aware of the choice between scarcity and abundance. The way you view the world, or the philosophy you operate under, plus your human life value determines every other aspect of your life, without exception. Scarcity produces consumers, while from abundance arise producers, which is vividly demonstrated in the next chapter.

Consumers try to hoard information and ideas for themselves. They believe it gives them some kind of competitive advantage. Producers freely mastermind and network with other producers because they believe in abundance which leads to connection and building a great network.

Action: want to find other producers? You are only one idea or one relationship away from the next level of prosperity. That is exactly why I created a Producer Power Hour Mastermind. You will find a free trial and other details at ProducerPowerHour.com.

This is how it looks on the Money Tree.™

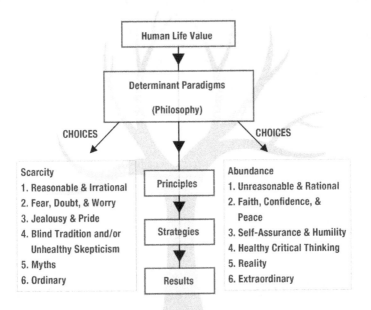

Chapter 4

Principles & Their Application
(As Determined By Our Paradigm)

Principles are timeless, universal truths, and five
principles of prosperity are outlined in this chapter. Consumers operate in scarcity and consume
more value than they create; producers operate
in abundance and create more value than they
consume. Consumers apply principles to their
demise; producers apply principles to serve and
prosper.

Principles are natural laws of the universe and
that hold true. Principles govern the universe
and determine the consequences of actions taken by
human beings. They are the structure, or the framework that provides the context of existence. Living in
accordance with correct principles leads to success;
violating principles leads to failure.

In this chapter, I will detail five principles of prosperity and outline how they are applied: application

based on the scarcity paradigm versus application based on the abundance paradigm.

5 Principles of Prosperity

1. People Have Intrinsic Value; Material Things Have None

How much are your material possessions worth? If you're like most people, you reasonably answered with a number. For our purposes let's say it's $500,000. But think about it—are your material possessions really worth $500,000 intrinsically? If those same possessions were in the middle of the Sahara desert, would they still be "worth" that? The value changes based on many factors, right? This is another way of saying that no material thing has intrinsic value; people give intrinsic value to material things. Your possessions are only worth what you're willing to receive in payment for them, and what other people are willing to pay for them.

Many people who own rental homes think that the home is the asset, and they are always worried that the tenant—who they think is the liability—is going to ruin their precious asset. The reality is just the opposite; people are the assets in any exchange, and material things are only useful as they relate to and serve human purposes.

2. Property Value is Derived From Human Life Value

Natural resources have only as much utility as people determine; they only have value as they are used to fulfill people's wants. Cell phones and computers were just dirt and metal until people applied their human life value to them. It is through human ingenuity and the application of ideas that we organize earthly resources to become material things.

People in scarcity spend their lives trying to amass property value (houses, cars, money, toys, etc.) while largely ignoring their human life value, without realizing that it is through their human life value that property value has any meaning or utility at all. What may be a horrible real estate investment for me might be a great deal for someone else. The difference is in our respective levels of human life value; the property is the same for both of us.

3. Value Follows Value

In a world of cause and effect, value is a cause and money is an effect. The seeming paradox of prosperity is that if we want to receive dollars (or any other form of value), the principled, effective way to receive is to stop thinking of the value we want, and instead, start providing value for other people in the way that they want it. The more value we create for others, the more value we receive in return. The prosperity in our lives is a direct reflection of the prosperity that we bring into the lives of others.

4. Wealth is Created Through Unequal Exchange

We all value things differently. If I were to sell you this book for $15, then what is the book worth to me and what is the book worth to you? You may think $15, but this is exactly wrong. We only give up something in an exchange when we value what we're receiving more than we value what we're giving up. Hence, there is no way to quantify an exact amount that the book or the $15 was worth to you or me. All I can conclusively say is that to you, the book was worth more than $15 and the $15 was worth less than the book; to me the book was worth less than $15 and the $15 was worth more than the book. We both walk away wealthier than before we made the transaction because we both have something that is worth more to us than before.

You only exchange when others have something that you value more than what you currently have. You never trade like-value for like-value because you have no incentive to trade like for like. You trade what you have for what you actually want more. This is how profit is made.

In a free market, the final sales price of any object is always an amount that the seller and the buyer both disagree that the object is worth. Therefore, exchange can only occur in an atmosphere of disagreement.

It must be clarified here that only the right exchanges for the right reasons create real wealth. In other words, if a person makes an exchange of money to receive heroine, is either party really wealthier because of that exchange? Absolutely not; they have both engaged in destroying their human life value.

Ideally, wealth is created by people living in Soul Purpose who exchange with others living in Soul Purpose. Soul Purpose allows you to specialize in those things that you are phenomenal at doing, that create real value in the world, and that bring you true joy. Where you have weaknesses, others are strong in their respective Soul Purposes. One of the best ways that you can create wealth is by aligning your value creation to your Soul Purpose and creating mutually beneficial exchanges with others who stick to their Soul Purpose.

5. The Evidence of Value

The way to know for certain if you have created real value for others is if you profit from that service. You profit when you get more out of a transaction—as you perceive—than you put into it, or that you value what you received more than what you gave. It must be understood that profit comes in many forms, the least of which is money; it can come simply through the good feeling you receive from service. Money is payment when you create value for a party that you don't know, and is therefore the most efficient method of exchange.

Consumers & Producers

Now that I have outlined these five principles of prosperity, I will explore how they are applied by individuals operating in scarcity versus those in abundance. I'll identify those living in scarcity as "consumers" and those living in abundance as "producers." Simply put, consumers create less value in the world than they take, and producers create more value than they take.

Living constantly in scarcity is what leads people to become consumers. consumers are characterized by the following traits, conditions, actions and perspectives:

Selfishness   Take and Manipulate
Victimhood   Belief that Profit is evidence
Irresponsibility   of exploitation
Win/Lose Transactions   Hoarding

Embracing an abundance mindset helps people to become producers. In contrast to consumers, producers are characterized by the following traits, conditions, actions, and perspectives:

Soul Purpose   Belief that Profit Equals
Heroism   Evidence of Value
Stewardship   Creation
Win/Win Transactions   Sharing
Giving and Serving

Selfishness vs. Soul Purpose

Consumers tend to be miserly and selfish, and they tend to bring others down as well. They are more concerned with what's in it for them now, rather than with what they can provide for others. They're constantly on the lookout for how they can benefit from relationships and transactions, rather than how they can provide value for others.

People can be consumers in certain areas of their life and not others. Are there any areas you are selfish or bringing people down? These are the areas you have given your power away to the Consumer Condition.

Producers are the responsible, innovative, and creative people who create all of the products and services that we buy and use. They are in touch with their personal mission, or their Soul Purpose, and this guides their choices. Like consumers, they also have their own wants, or self-interest, but how they go about fulfilling those wants is fundamentally different than consumers. Producers understand that it is in their best interest to help others get what they want.

Are there areas where you are uplifting and inspiring? These are the areas you are empowered to live in the Producer Paradigm.

Victimhood vs. Heroism

Consumers seek to blame everything and anything for the things that go wrong in their lives including their boss, their company, the government, their spouses, etc. They think that the world is out to get them and they depend on others for their happiness and well-being. Because of their unwillingness to find power internally, they are waiting for external circumstances to determine their path.

Producers choose to be heroes, regardless of external circumstances they face. They rise above challenges by taking responsibility for how they choose to deal with them. They understand the power of choice and exercise it wisely. Through a willingness to be responsible for their circumstance, producers look internally to find power and pave the path to prosperity.

Insight

In June of 2006, a plane crash killed two of my business partners, Les McGuire and Ray Hooper. I was overwhelmed with both the sense of loss combined with the feeling of responsibility to take care of Les and Ray's office and clients. Over months, this led to a lot of discontentment and scarcity in my life.

I realized then that I had a choice to make: I could either be a victim of the circumstance, or I could transcend it and practice what I had been preaching to people. I had been teaching people to love their life, and now it was becoming difficult for me to even get up in the morning. I chose to love my life.

The first thing I did was to stay at home for about 30 days. I spent time with my family, I read a lot, I meditated, I focused on getting my thoughts right and being happy again. I quickly found reservoirs of creativity that I had never before experienced at that level. It was during this time that I created the Freedom FastTrack process, which has now helped thousands of people find greater joy, purpose, and success in their lives.

I had a choice to become internal and align with principle. Thankfully, I made the powerful choice at that time. It wasn't easy, but through my increased perspective, I now see that I probably wouldn't have created many of the things that exist in my business today, had it not been for that event and that choice. I also have been blessed to see the divinity in difficult situations, as that is what leads us to grow.

Irresponsibility vs. Stewardship

Consumers avoid responsibility whenever possible. When bad things happen, it's someone else's fault (in their view). They rarely take good care of the blessings they have received, and when they do, it's from a selfish standpoint because they think that their material things actually belong to them, rather than to God.

Producers understand that, materially speaking, they came into this life with nothing, they will leave with nothing, and everything in between is a stewardship from God to be taken care of. They don't feel a sense of ownership; they understand that nothing belongs to them and is merely a temporary stewardship. They take excellent care of their stewardships without falling prey to the idea that things actually belong to them.

Win/Lose vs. Win/Win

Because they're so heavily influenced by scarcity, consumers believe that all economic transactions result in one person winning and one person losing. They're always on the lookout for a "good deal," which translates as them being able to win at the expense of others. It also creates favorable conditions for envy, theft, and deception as people work to accumulate more than others through destructive competition.

Producers understand that, in the absence of deception and/or coercion, every single economic transaction is a win for all parties involved. They know that we only engage in exchange when we value what we're receiving more than what we're giving up. Because we have different perspectives and abilities, two people can both win from a transaction that is willingly entered into.

Win/win transactions are especially enabled when all parties are willing to look beyond cash and consider other forms of exchange. For example, one of my friends, Stephen Palmer, benefited enormously from an exchange of human life value. Stephen is a writer, and we needed a lot of writing done for part of the FastTrack program. The portion Stephen was writing for was

a $10,000 investment at that time. He completed all of the writing for the program, and in exchange, was able to complete the program without having to come up with $10,000 cash.

The benefits on both sides far outweighed $10,000 in cash. When asked if he would have preferred $10,000 over going through the program, Stephen says, "Not a chance." To him, the benefits of the program were worth far more than the money. And on our end, Stephen was a huge asset because he was familiar with the content. If we had used any other writer, we would have spent far more time and effort educating him or her on the material, which would have cost us much more than $10,000 in the long run.

Although no cash was exchanged, we won by getting all of our written materials completed, and Stephen won by going through the program. We each got more out of the exchange than we perceived we were putting into it.

Take & Manipulate vs. Give & Serve

Consumers are more concerned with what they can take from others than with what they can give. Whenever they have a hard time getting what they want, they resort to manipulation and deceit.

Producers are more concerned with giving than with receiving. They know that the best way for them to be happy is to serve others. Producers lift, bless, serve, and contribute to everything good in the world. They always leave things better than they found them, even if they weren't responsible for the destruction that they fix.

Insight

When I was a teenager, I went camping with my Dad. On the way home, we passed an empty campsite that was full of garbage. I was anxious to get home, but my Dad stopped the truck, pulled over, and began picking up the garbage.

A little bit frustrated and impatient, I asked him why he was cleaning up a mess that he didn't create. He responded that as a member of the community, he felt a responsibility for creating a great place to live, regardless of who made the messes to clean up.

This was a pivotal moment in my life when I learned that responsible people always give more to their community and the world than they take from it.

Profit = Exploitation vs. Profit = Evidence of Value Creation

Consumers think that any time anyone profits, that some kind of exploitation was involved. They think that the higher the profits, the greater the exploitation.

Producers understand that it is a natural law of the universe that we prosper when we create value. They love and enjoy profit because they understand that it is only through value creation that any individual can truly profit.

When I wrote Killing Sacred Cows, I put massive amounts of human life value into the book. I packaged my human life value in such a way that others could benefit from without me having to be physically, personally, and immediately present.

Anyone who buys the book does so because they perceive profit by doing so; they believe that they are receiving more value from the book than they are giving up in cash. There's no exploitation involved—just voluntary exchange resulting in profit on both sides. And I profited immensely from the book and the business and relationships that it continues to generate. That profit represents value creation.

Hoarding vs. Sharing

Because of their constant fear of loss, consumers hoard. From knowledge to material resources. They typically don't like sharing information with others because they don't want anyone to benefit from their knowledge. They hoard money and hold tight to their material goods.

Producers share their blessings with as many people as possible through responsible and sustainable means. It is the key that unlocks healthy relationships and is an axis to value creation. Rather than hoarding, producers are stewards that utilize resources to increase their ability to produce.

Applying the Principles

What does all of this about consumers and producers have to do with principles? Simply put, these two types of people view and apply the principles of prosperity very differently.

Consumers think that material things are assets, and so they use, manipulate, and deceive people to get more material things. Producers know that people are the only true assets, and they use material things to serve people.

Comparing our lives to a tree, consumers have rotten roots and go around complaining about their lack of fruit, or that their fruit is bitter, while they ignore their roots. Due to jealousy, they spend time wanting the fruits of others—and usually without wanting to put forth any effort. Producers, on the other hand, focus on developing their human life value and enjoy the fruits of property value.

Consumers live in a world of scarcity, where every transaction is, by default, win-lose. If there are finite resources, you can only become wealthier at the expense of someone else. And when you think about it, how long can an economic model like that last? What are the inevitable results of that model? Is it any wonder that when economic theories based on scarcity—such as socialism—are applied they always fail and result in misery? Producers understand that every transaction must be win-win for it to be a principled exchange. Even if there is temporary or short-term benefit, a producer will not engage in a transaction that is losing for the other party.

Consumers are self-proclaimed martyrs who claim that they would be wealthy if they weren't so "nice." They make exchanges that are a loss to them in order to maintain their martyr status; they want to make sure that others know what "good" people they are. But this is selfishness and irresponsibility, plain and simple. There's nothing virtuous or enlightened about priding oneself on how much they lose so that others can gain. In fact, it's a violation of principle if any exchange results in a net loss for any one of the parties involved.

Summary

Our paradigm determines how we view the world and other people. The scarcity paradigm leads people to think and act like consumers, while the abundance paradigm leads people to think and act like producers. In other words, our philosophy determines how we understand and apply principles of prosperity.

This is how it looks on the Money Tree model.

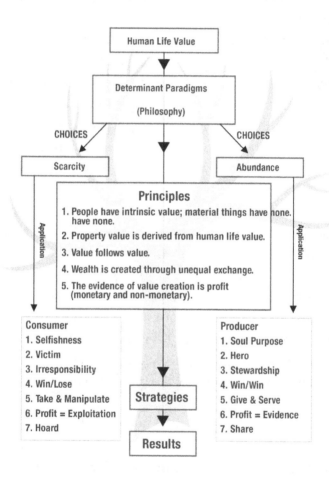

Chapter 5

Financial Strategies: Accumulation versus Utilization

The results of scarcity are false security and a loss of freedom. The results of abundance are true security and expansive freedom. From scarcity and abundance flow all desires, actions, and political and economic structures.

The types of strategies we use and how we apply them come as a direct result of our human life value, our paradigm, and how we view and use principles. Scarcity leads to the Consumer Condition, which in turn leads people to apply certain types of strategies that are opposite to those utilized in abundance through the Producer Paradigm.

Accumulation Versus Utilization

Different types of strategies may be classified in two main categories: accumulation and utilization. Scarcity and the Consumer Condition lead to strategies based on accumulation, while abundance and the Producer Paradigm lead to strategies based on utilization.

Accumulation, which is the theory of wealth taught by retirement planners, says that the way to build wealth is to save and accumulate as much money as needed to live off of the interest. It's fundamentally based in scarcity, it limits our productivity, it avoids personal responsibility, and it places value in material things, products, and strategies, rather than in people. Accumulation is fundamentally product and strategy driven, rather than based in an understanding of the root of prosperity: human life value.

Utilization, on the other hand, says that the way to prosper is to make an inventory of all one's current resources—both human life value and property value resources—and then become creative about maximizing their productivity in the present. It's based on what you can do right now, today, to be as productive and valuable as possible, instead of waiting 30 years to enjoy life. Utilization is driven by the understanding that one's human life value is infinitely more important than products and strategies.

Accumulation is characterized by the following conditions and strategies:

Dependence	Retirement
Micro Perspective	Budget and Constraint
Do-it-Yourself	Risk
Price Sensitive	Unsecured Investments

Compound Interest   Term Insurance
Dollar-Cost-Average   Qualified Retirement Plans
Self-Insurance   Diversification

In contrast, utilization is characterized by the following conditions and strategies:

Personal Responsibility   Investor DNA
Macro Perspective   Collateralized Investments
Synergize   Velocity
Cost & Value   Control Terms
Soul Purpose   Maximum Insurance
Increase Production   Permanent Insurance
Cash Flow   Real Estate & Business
Certainty   Focus
Risk Management

Insight

I started as a mutual fund and life insurance salesman in 1998 and 1999. It wasn't about investing in yourself, expressing Soul Purpose, building cash flow or anything that you would read on the abundance side of this book; I fell trap to the accumulation perspective of life.

I thought that if I could just save my self rich by cutting back, delaying, and sacrificing, I could build up a big reserve that one day they would pay off and I would be blessed and have a great life. The one day, some day type of thinking. I had given my power up to a market that I couldn't control and marketing that didn't match the result people experienced with their money—the accumulation philosophy. The irony of this thought process is that in the moment of my hoarding I was miserable, and so were the people in my life.

A major paradigm shift can be demonstrated with the New Testament in the book of Matthew chapter twenty-five. This chapter expresses a parable about three stewards who received talents. Two of them utilized their talents and were blessed, while the third, out of fear and ignorance, attempted to accumulate his talent by burying it in the ground.

The first two stewards ended with growth and abundance, while the third suffered death and scarcity. I realized then that my days of hiding my talents were over, and that expressing and utilizing the gifts God had given me to bless the lives of those around me and myself would be the only way I was going to live.

Dependence vs. Personal Responsibility

What does all of this about consumers and producers have to do with principles? Simply put, these two types of people view and apply the principles of prosperity very differently.

The primary purpose of accumulation theory practitioners is to get you to buy a product and leave the rest up to them. The way it is taught, all a person has to do is put regular payments into 401(k)s or mutual funds and the market will take care of the rest. In other words, those that buy into it are almost entirely dependent on the things outside of their control including the market, the viability and trustworthiness of companies who take their money, and the government. By its very nature, the success or failure of accumulation is based on things external to the individual.

The starting point of utilization is you, the individual investor. Not a product, not a strategy, not a technique—you. Utilization requires that an investor take full responsibility for everything in their financial life. Such investors understand that their success is dependent upon them as individuals and not on any magic product or other factor. Responsible investors aren't tossed about by every whim of the market; they make their own markets. When things go wrong, responsible investors look inward to what they can do themselves to solve the problem, while dependent investors look outside of themselves to place blame. They invest in themselves. They invest in things they know. They are ok sitting on cash when the time isn't right to deploy assets. They automatically save, but deliberately invest-avoiding the clichés pitched by the so-called financial experts that are more salesman than strategist. Ultimately they understand they are their greatest asset. Not a stock, bond or piece of real estate. It is their ability to create value.

Micro vs. Macro

A micro perspective of finances takes specific aspects of a person's plan and views those aspects alone, without considering their relationship with or effect on any other part of the plan. This is how accumulation theory advisors create and implement financial plans. For example, in a micro perspective, if a person wanted insurance they would consider insurance alone and would most likely try to find the cheapest insurance as possible. Or let's say they wanted to start a small investment account. Most product-driven accumulation theorists would automatically advise them to do something like open a mutual fund account and contribute to it monthly. Without more context and information, this approach ignores many crucial factors in the decision.

A macro perspective, on the other hand, looks at a person's plan in its entirety and aids them in making holistic decisions that take all factors into consideration. Every financial decision affects every other aspect of one's plan including, but not limited to, cash flow, tax consequences, legal and liability issues, loan interest, risk factors, etc. Ultimately, a macro perspective views the plan in the context of how it will impact the person's life and contribute to Soul Purpose. All thoughts and actions have consequences, and the utilization theory of wealth considers all consequences of a person's financial decisions by using a macro perspective.

Do-it-Yourself vs. Synergize

These two concepts are actually perfect examples of micro versus macro. The micro, accumulation perspective teaches that in order to "save money," people should do as many things for themselves as possible. They should change their own oil, fix their own car, make all home repairs, etc.

The utilization perspective teaches that a person should find the areas where they are unique, find the most enjoyment, and where they can offer the most value, and then synergize with others to do the things that are not a part of their Soul Purpose. With utilization, we learn that we can dramatically increase our production by focusing our time and efforts on where we can create the most value (leverage), and utilize the abilities of others in other areas of our life.

For example, suppose a person needs an oil change in their vehicle. An average oil change costs $29.95. Looking at this from a micro perspective, it would appear that this person will save $29.95 by changing their own oil. However, the macro perspective considers every other factor at play. What if we knew that this person made $50 per hour on average in their career, and it would take them one hour to change their oil? Or if they are not able to spend time with their family. How does this change the picture? Now it's clear to see that this person is actually losing $20.05 to change their oil or missing out on valuable memories that cannot be replaced.

Price vs. Cost & Value

Cutting coupons and looking for "good deals" are standard procedures in the accumulation theory. People become so obsessed with the prices of items that they largely ignore the value and cost aspects of the decision.

By value I mean the utility or usefulness that any item has in your life, regardless of its price. By cost I mean all of the initially unseen factors beyond price in the decision making process.

There is much more to consider when making financial decisions than price alone. Cost and value are much more important considerations than price, as they determine the long-term success or failure of purchasing decisions much more than price.

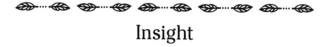

Insight

I remember thinking that it was pretty expensive. Then the thought occurred to me, "What if I had to make this thing? What would the cost be of me having to build a bike by myself?" Think of all the human life value that goes into producing one bicycle. It would take me a lifetime to build alone what others were able to create for a relatively small price, even less than the $4,000 they charged me for the bike. And we both profited from the exchange.

Too often, though, all we see is the price tag of an item, while failing to see the cost of us creating it ourselves.

Through interdependence and synergy, we can utilize the Soul Purpose of others to get much higher quality goods and services than we can provide for ourselves. Are there areas where you're trying to save but it's at the expense of production? And would you actually be able to produce more if you focused on the production rather than just the savings?

Retirement vs. Soul Purpose

When you strip it bare to its fundamental root, the traditional concept of retirement means that those who retire literally become economically dead. The idea is that we work hard for 30 years, accumulate a "nest egg," stop working, and live off the interest from our accumulated funds.

There are several problems with this idea. First of all, it makes us think that we have to wait 30 years to enjoy life and be financially free. Secondly, it causes many people to stay in jobs and careers that they don't like, that don't energize them, and that aren't the full expression of their unique abilities. And finally, if we were doing what we were born to do and loving life, why would we ever want to quit?

Soul Purpose, in contrast to retirement, is the idea that there is something inside of every individual that is the ultimate expression of who they are, of what they can contribute to the world, and that is aligned with Divine Will. By embracing Soul Purpose, you stop waiting for life and freedom to come to you; you go get them. You don't remain in situations that drain your energy and inhibit your ability to produce greater value. And when you're energized through the process, you can't conceive of ever not living your mission.

Reduce Expenses vs. Increase Production

Most accumulation-based books and advisors teach you to decrease your expenses as much as possible in order to save more money for retirement. While there is definitely merit to decreasing expenses, especially in a consumption-driven culture where most people are borrowing to consume, I generally take issue with how this is applied so dogmatically. The problem is that it takes people's focus, effort, and energy away from the bigger picture.

Living within your means is great advice, as long as you also look at increasing your means by applying your human life value. Instead of merely decreasing expenses, one can invest money into education or even spend time reading and engaging in powerful conversations. The Producer Power Hour, for example, is a proven system with powerful tools to help individuals increase production through education. The more you discover and experience your Soul Purpose, the more possibility there is for production.

For example, suppose a couple sat down to review their finances and determined that they weren't saving enough. The traditional solution would be for them to comb through their budget and find things they could cut out of their life. Let's say that by doing so they are able to decrease their expenses by $200 per month, but it takes them four hours over two days to figure this out.

What could happen in their life if they spent those four hours on finding ways to increase their production and cash flow instead? How different would that conversation be? What epiphanies would they experience? Is it possible that in the same time they could increase their monthly income by $400? Furthermore, assuming they actually implemented strategies to increase their production, what are the quantum, long-term effects of that decision? What if they focused that time on starting a business? Then, because they start a business, they drastically increase their knowledge of marketing strategies, accounting practices, customer relations, etc. Their human life value is exponentially worth more now because they spent more time increasing production instead of reducing expenses.

We see a tax savings of 11,340 dollars per $500,000 of revenue for business owners that learn our 5-part tax efficiency framework. Or $2,484 per month for those that go through Cash Flow Optimization. These are savings without sacrifice. They focus on financial savvy and intelligence leading to keeping more of what you make rather than missing out on experiences or enjoyment of life in the name of retirement.

Be more efficient within your means first, expand your means second and be mindful of living within your means as well. This three part formula takes into consideration being a producer, proper steward and enjoying life along the way.

While reducing expenses can be an important part of a whole plan, ultimately a person's macro plan should be based on spending time and effort figuring out how they can increase their production.

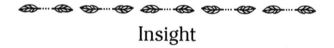

Insight

When I was 22, I thought the road to wealth was to reduce all my expenses and live in an apartment and save a whole bunch of money. I thought that I could call myself successful if I just had a lot of money in the bank.

It took awhile for me to realize that I was not the type of person that you would want to spend a lot of time with because of my scarcity mindset and habits. You wouldn't want to be waiting on me at a restaurant because I wasn't going to leave a big tip, for fear that it would hurt my precious net worth. I was going to drive something that was broken down and maybe not the safest vehicle because it might hurt my net worth to have something else. My wife and I lived in an apartment even though we owned many investment real estate properties.

Risk vs. Certainty

If you've ever worked with an advisor in the accumulation camp, you've probably taken a risk profile to determine how much risk you can handle. The idea, of course, is that the higher returns you want to enjoy, the more willing you must be to take on risk. This is perhaps the most backwards, illogical teaching of the entire accumulation theory, yet so few people are able to see it for what it is. When we break it down logically, does it make any sense that in order to increase our chance of winning we must also increase our chance of losing?

Through utilization, you learn that the way to prosper is to decrease your risk as much as possible. Because of the prevalence of advice from retirement planners, most people balk at this idea because they've been trained to equate low risk investments with low returns (i.e. Certificates of Deposits, Money Market accounts, bonds, etc.). However, there are numerous risk mitigation strategies that can dramatically increase your investment returns. The more certain you can make any investment, the greater chance you have of profiting. Risk-taking is a strategy for people in scarcity who rely upon simple luck for success.

The fact is that financial institutions have a vested interest in you believing this. Why? Because they are using it as a technique to get you to take on their risk! It's a risk-transference, insurance strategy for them. What's even more interesting is that the same institutions do exactly the opposite with their money than what they teach you to do with your money. They're not taking risks; they're getting end consumers to take on their risks for them.

For example, if you apply for a mortgage, some ways that the bank will mitigate their risks are to do the following:

Check your credit.

Secure their investments with collateral. Typically require a down payment.

Control the interest rate.

Control the payment.

Control the time period for each investment.

Impose pre-payment penalties.

Verify your work history and income.

Cover all of their investments with insurance (and interestingly enough, they have you buy it).

Have an exit strategy that allows them to be profitable, or to at least return their initial capital, in almost any scenario.

Collateralize their investment (see below) so that if you default on the loan, they can foreclose on the house and resell it.

Transfer their risks to the borrower in any way possible.

Unsecured Investments vs. Collateralized Investments

When a person "invests" in a mutual fund, what security do they have if the mutual fund fails to produce a positive return? Of course the answer is that they have no security at all. The mutual fund does not guarantee any results, and if they lose money, they have no recourse to gain it back.

Abundance and utilization-based investors seek downside protection. One way to do this is through collateral. Within a financial context collateral is an asset that secures a payment obligation. Collateral can come in many forms including real estate, cars, jewelry, percentages of ownership in companies, percentages of sales agreements, legal documents, ownership in intellectual property, etcetera. For example, in the case of a mortgage, the house serves as the collateral for the mortgage loan. This way, the bank is secured against the default risk of the borrower not being able to meet the interest payments. In case of default, the bank can sell the house and get its money (or at least a part of it) back.

Almost every product sold by retirement planners is not collateralized in any way. On the other hand, utilization teaches that every investment you make should have some form of risk mitigation and downside protection.

Having said this, it must be stressed that securing collateral is but one risk mitigation technique, and not something to be excited about or depend on. It's one of the last things to consider when it comes to making an investment. The primary focus of your investment strategies are whether or not the people with whom you are dealing can be trusted, and if it is a solid value proposition.

In other words, don't make investments simply because they're collateralized, and you're hoping that the person defaults so that you can take the asset. Make investments with people of integrity and that create real value for others so that you'll never have to exercise foreclosure proceedings to secure the collateral involved.

Compound Interest vs. Velocity

You've more than likely heard of compound interest being "miraculous," but what is it? Compound interest is the concept of adding accumulated interest back to the principal, so that interest is earned on interest from that moment on. For example, suppose you owe someone $1,000, with an annual interest rate of 12%, for a monthly payment of $10. If instead of taking the payment you decide to compound the interest, in the second month the person owes you $1,010, and the interest is then calculated from that new balance. In the next month, the new balance would be $1,020.10, and so on.

Generally speaking, the reason for compounding interest is based on the scarcity construct of accumulation. It takes long periods of time to pay off and still leads to people living lives of mediocrity and hoarding resources for fear of losing them. It limits the productive capacity of every individual who engages in it. It also exposes them to many conditions that can negatively impact them, such as inflation, volatility, and taxes, with little or no way of mitigating those risks.

Also, what happens if your calculations are based on a steady 8% annual return, but your investment account actually fluctuates between -15% and +15%? The entire calculation is drastically thrown off, and compound interest becomes obsolete. In other words, my problem with compound interest isn't actually with the concept itself; rather, our problem is how financial institutions get people to buy products based on the concept, when the actual effect is much different than how it looks on paper.

Utilization theorists teach the concept of velocity, instead of compound interest. While compound interest trains a person to hold money for long periods of time, velocity teaches that the faster money circulates the more wealth is created.

Simply put, velocity means to greatly increase output with little or no additional input. We can velocitize one of three ways: 1) through exchange, and 2) through simultaneous use 3) efficiency.

First, velocity is created through exchange when we increase the speed of financial transactions. It's the difference between profit margin and turnover.

If the price of any inventory is extremely high there may be a great profit margin, but by lowering the price more of a good is sold and would create greater turnover and therefore velocity. Second, the idea of velocity through simultaneous use is to find multiple purposes for every dollar that goes into an investment. For example, if a person puts money in a savings account to be used as an emergency fund, every dollar going into that account serves only one purpose. However, there are other investments that provide multiple uses for each individual dollar, things such as control, flexibility, rate of return, risk mitigation, tax protection, liability protection, disability protection, and death protection.

Another example is that when I speak at events, we always film and record the event. This gives us the ability to leverage and velocitize that same content with very little increased input. We can put it into video or audio form, or transcribe the audio and create articles from it, for example.

Here's the bottom line difference between compound interest (at least how it's taught and the actual result of the practice) and velocity: compound interest teaches to put money away and let it sit, while velocity focuses on cash flow increasing output without increasing our input through moving money rapidly and find multiple uses for it.

Dollar-Cost-Average vs. Control Terms

Dollar-cost-averaging is yet another trick that financial institutions use to get our money. Here's the idea of dollar-cost-averaging: Suppose a person invests $100 per month into a mutual fund, with a current price of $10 per share. The first month, their $100 contribution buys them 10 shares. The next month, the share price goes up to $20, so their $100 contribution buys them only five shares. In month three, the share price drops to $5 per share, so they are able to buy 20 shares. The average cost per share over the three months was $11.66. However, this person only paid an average of $8.57 per share. Through dollar-cost-averaging, as a person contributes a steady monthly amount to an investment and as the investment price rises and falls, the person buys at an average price instead of possibly when it is high.

Now on the surface that may seem great. However, when we really analyze it we find just one more tool that gets people to give their money to financial institutions in steady, recurring amounts and keep it with those institutions for long periods of time without the thinking process to determine if it is working or achieving the investor's objective. Keep in mind that this is in investments that are not collateralized, that the "investor" has no way of controlling and has no way of mitigating risk and guaranteeing any return.

The utilization perspective helps you to be an active participant in determining the terms of investments, rather than being a passive subject to the whims of the market. The terms of investments are every component of the transaction beyond the price.

For example, suppose a home is for sale with a price of $300,000. If you were to buy the home using a 30-year mortgage with an interest rate of 6%, the monthly payment would be $1,798. However, after visiting with the seller you find that she is very motivated and will let you move into the home using a lease option contract.

A lease option contract allows you to lease a home, while locking in the current price should you decide to purchase the home during your lease period. Using such a contract allows for much more flexible terms than just the price of a cash-at-closing deal.

After negotiating with the seller, you are able to lock in a price of $275,000 on an 18-month contract, with no money down, and a monthly payment of $1,500. The benefits to you now include that you did not have to use your credit to control the property, your monthly payment is less than it would have been had you gotten a mortgage, you may be able to sublease it for a positive cash flow, and you lock in the price for an 18-month period, which may also allow the home to appreciate.

When it comes to risk mitigation strategies, there is one critical difference between accumulation and utilization: Risk mitigation using accumulation amounts can be achieved to a degree with stop-loss mechanisms. Most people don't hear about these from their advisors since it may mean that if the stop-loss is trigged it may mean a loss of commission plus the accumulation theory states the longer you wait, the better your chance of realizing a return. Risk mitigation using utilization, on the other hand, means to immediately control the terms of the investments we enter into and do anything to guarantee a return at the time of purchase. In other words, accumulation says that you make a profit when you sell, and utilization says that you make a profit when you buy.

Instead of asking where the best place to invest is, ask how you can be a better investor? What types of investments make sense based upon your knowledge? What do you find yourself studying or where do you have superior intellect?

How can you protect the downside? What level of guarantee does the investment have? Does it create cash flow immediately? Does it lead you toward financial independence through recurring revenue?

Self-Insurance vs. Maximum Insurance

The scarcity-driven accumulation theory has come up with a concept riddled with fallacies called self-insurance. The idea of self-insurance is that a person can accumulate enough cash and other assets so that they can stop paying insurance premiums, and when a loss occurs, they can use their own money to make up for the loss.

The problem is that the concept itself is a contradiction of terms; it is impossible for self-insurance to even exist. The purpose of insurance is to provide indemnification for losses and to transfer risk. Simply put, indemnification means that a sum is paid by one person or institution (A) to another (B) by way of compensation for a loss suffered by B. The dictionary definition of indemnify is: 1) To compensate for damage or loss sustained, expense incurred, etc., and 2) To guard or secure against anticipated loss; give security against future damage or liability.

With self-insurance, a person has no way of providing indemnification for losses; any time they incur a loss, no money outside of their own resources comes in to replace what was lost.

Through insurance coverage, a person can guarantee indemnification for losses for a relatively small cost. This is done because insurance companies are able to pool risks and thus offer large benefits to individuals because so many others are contributing to the pool.

Utilization teaches that the best way for a person to reduce their insurance costs is to secure as much insurance as possible. It may sound counter-intuitive, yet it is completely logical. Consider two people whom we will call Tom and Bob. Tom and Bob are neighbors and their homes are both worth $200,000. Tom has $200,000 in the bank and believes in self-insurance, and so he carries no homeowners insurance. Bob also has $200,000 in the bank, but carries a full homeowners insurance policy. Both houses burn down, and the homeowners both decide to rebuild. Which person ends up paying more for their insurance? Obviously Tom, because his "self-insurance" cost him a full $200,000 to replace his home. Not only does Bob get to keep his $200,000 in the bank, but he is also able to rebuild his home through his insurance proceeds.

The topic of insurance brings us back to the concept of risk mitigation: accumulation theorists do not understand and apply appropriate risk mitigation techniques (in fact they advocate high risk), while utilization theorists understand and apply the power of certainty. Insurance is one of the most important ways a person can provide certainty in their life.

Term Insurance vs. Permanent Insurance

Term life insurance—the insurance sold by many, if not most, accumulation advisors—is insurance that provides a death benefit for a certain period of time. Unlike permanent life insurance, term does not accrue a cash value within the policy, and has no living benefits. Permanent life insurance policies are designed to provide coverage for the duration of a person's lifetime, and not a specified term only. They carry a cash value that accrues with premiums paid, and provide many benefits that a policyholder has access to while they are living.

The main reason that many financial strategists sell term is because term insurance is supposedly cheaper than permanent insurance. The problem with this is that, when viewed from a macro perspective, this is blatantly false, and furthermore, permanent insurance provides much more certainty and reduces much more risk than does term.

The differences between term and permanent insurance are too many to fully describe in this short book. The best resources to learn more is Wealth Factory.com/Rockefellers/book or CashFlowBanking .com.

For now, here are the main points to understand: The accumulation theory promotes term insurance because it is cheap (at least from a micro perspective), because they believe in the false concept of self-insurance, and because they fail to see the link between human life value and property value. The utilization theory promotes permanent life insurance because it is actually far more cost effective than other types of insurance in a macro sense, because they understand the inestimable value of certainty, and because they understand human life value and how to protect it.

Qualified Retirement Plans vs. Soul Purpose, Real Estate & Business

Qualified retirement plans are retirement vehicles created by the government such as 401(k)s and IRAs. Accumulation theorists, representing financial institutions, are huge proponents of these plans. They like them because people can put them on automatic withdrawal, they are supposedly affordable, and they have supposed tax advantages (although these are misunderstood and taught wrong more often than not).

Utilization theorists don't prefer them, however, because those participating have very few ways to mitigate their risk exposure, extremely limited ability to guarantee a profit, limited access during the deferral period, and very little control. Furthermore, the purported tax advantages of qualified retirement plans don't actually result in many real advantages, when understood fully and considered from a macro perspective. This is why in utilization I prefer Cash Flow Banking (CashFlowBanking.com), real estate (if aligned with your Investor DNA), and businesses.

Through real estate and business, you can use your human life value to influence the terms, generate profits, provide immediate cash flow, collateralize your investments, and velocitize your money. Furthermore, both of these provide far more ability for you to realize your Soul Purpose, which is the end of all investing in the first place.

Diversify vs. Focus

Diversification is the idea that by spreading your money into several different investments, you reduce your risk. If one or a few investments lose money, says the theory, the chances are that not all of your investments will lose money at the same time.

This idea is commonly used in the accumulation theory through mutual funds. Mutual funds are investment pools where a fund buys stocks or bonds in multiple companies, and then investors can buy shares of that fund. What this amounts to however, is simply an ineffective risk mitigation tool for unsophisticated investors. What it really means is that those investing really have no idea what each individual company within the fund is doing and how they are a sound investment, and that they're just hoping and praying that the fund will go up in value. Frankly put, this is gambling, not investing.

True investors don't practice unconscious diversification; they practice educated focus. The most successful investors in the world, from Robert Kiyosaki, to Andrew Carnegie, to Warren Buffett, have always taught focus over diversification. Through focus, you don't have to rely on hope and market factors completely outside of our control; you can be personally responsible, educated, and make wise choices that you are certain will result in a positive return.

Summary

Accumulation strategies flow from a scarcity paradigm, they are based on dependence upon institutions and factors outside of the control of most people, they are made from a micro perspective of finances, they subject investors to multiple and considerable risks, and leave investors with very little control.

On the contrary, utilization strategies flow from abundance, they are based upon responsibility, they are made from a macro perspective of finances, they allow investors to mitigate their risk, and provide investors with more control of financial results.

Increasing wealth, abundance and results starts with accountability. Without a structure of support, inspiration, or someone to hold you accountable to what you say you want for your life or what you are going to do can lead to procrastination, stagnation or lost potential. The Producer Power Hour Mastermind has others just like you on the path of financial independence an abundance mindset.

If you want to be held accountable to building a better and more prosperous future, visit Producer PowerHour.com.

See how it looks on the Money Tree model on the next page.

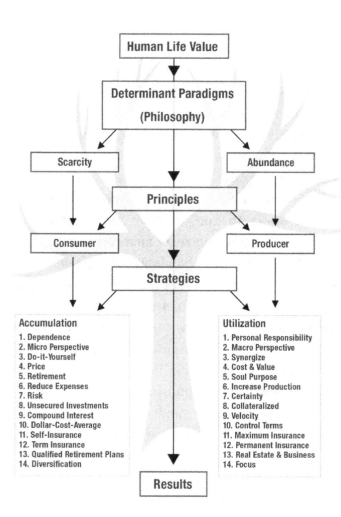

Chapter 6

End Results: Security versus Freedom

Accumulation strategies flow from scarcity and are practiced by consumers. Utilization strategies flow from abundance and are practiced by producers. Various strategies compared and contrasted to provide a revolutionary financial perspective and give direction on how to apply philosophy and principles.

As we have begun to see, the philosophies of scarcity and abundance create certain mindsets that lead to the application of specific strategies. These strategies lead to predictable results. This chapter will explore and discuss these results and their personal, economic, and political implications.

Security Versus Freedom

Simply put, scarcity leads to the Consumer Condition, which leads to accumulation strategies, which lead to a financially, spiritually, and mentally impoverished false sense of security and the loss of real freedom. Abundance leads to the Producer Paradigm, which leads to utilization strategies, which in turn lead to expansive freedom and true security. Let's now discuss some best and worst case scenarios for each of these types of results.

Best Case Scenarios

At a personal level, the best-case scenario for financial security is net worth, while for freedom it's cash flow. In the realm of political economy, the best case result for scarcity and security is either capitalism and/or democratic socialism. The best case result for abundance and freedom is free enterprise.

Net Worth vs. Cash Flow

A person's net worth is their assets minus their liabilities. There are various ways to determine what constitutes an asset, but the simplest definition is anything that can be liquidated for cash.

For example, suppose a person has a home with a market value of $250,000 with a mortgage of $200,000, a car that could sell for $15,000 with a loan balance of $10,000, miscellaneous items totaling $20,000, and a credit card balance of $8,000. To calculate their net worth, we add up their assets, add up their liabilities, and then subtract the liabilities from the assets to get the total. In this case, their total net worth is $67,000.

Assets		Liabilities	
Home:	$250,000	Mortgage:	$200,000
Car:	$15,000	Auto Loan:	$10,000
Misc.:	$20,000	Credit Card:	$8,000
Total:	$285,000	Total:	$218,000

The accumulation theory calculates a person's financial success based on net worth. This is why so many books exist that teach people to become "millionaires," or to have a net worth of $1 million or more.

The utilization theory puts much less emphasis on net worth and says that cash flow is the single best indicator of a person's financial success. Here's why: Suppose a person owns a piece of commercial real estate worth $1 million on paper, but it sits vacant with no tenants and thus produces no income. On paper, this person is a millionaire, yet their net worth does little good for them because it does not produce an income. Now, do they have the ability to produce an income with their net worth-based asset? Yes, but until that cash flow is realized, the asset is nothing but potential value, not real value.

Unless it can be leveraged and utilized to produce cash flow, net worth is a relatively worthless measurement of wealth. Cash flow, or income, is the best way to determine a person's financial health and success. Furthermore, the highest level of cash flow is portfolio income, or income derived from investments that require little time and effort from the investor.

The best case scenario for those who practice accumulation is net worth. They may have a big number to show on a piece of paper, yet they still live largely in scarcity because they're so afraid to utilize the principal of their nest egg. They don't understand powerful strategies involving permanent life insurance and therefore they cannot spend down their principal without losing their monthly income in the form of dividend and interest payments. Their main goal is to preserve their nest egg and live off the interest. At times they may feel secure, but they are far from free.

The best case scenario for those who practice utilization is a high portfolio income. They can start living their Soul Purpose today with the cash flow. Not only are they more secure in actuality than those who subscribe to the accumulation theory, but they also have more freedom. With these resources they have time to develop and realize their Soul Purpose and make a great contribution to the world. Their contribution is not limited by money or time.

Capitalism & Democratic Socialism vs. Free Enterprise

I'll warn you upfront that some may find this next section confronting and possibly even difficult to read. However, I urge you to spend time digesting and understanding it, as these concepts are so critical to our freedom, both as individuals and as a nation. These are the literal results of the two competing philoso-phies of scarcity and abundance, and unless we can fully grasp the import of this, we can never fully grasp why choosing abundance is so critical to the survival of any society.

We define capitalism as an economic system where investment and ownership of the means of production, distribution, and exchange of wealth is made and main-tained chiefly by private individuals or corporations. However, contrary to free enterprise, which treats all individuals and institutions equally before the law, capitalism is catalyzed and supported by a legal struc-ture which treats individuals and business entities unequally before the law. Under capitalism, the gov-ernment favors those with capital to the detriment of those with little or no capital.

While this is definitely better than outright social-ism or communism, as corporations receive special treatment from government, this eventually and inev-itably leads to destructive monopolization and con-glomeration. Economic power equates political power and this monopolization concentrates too much power in the hands of too few.

U.S. A 2012 study by Edward N. Wolff at New York University concluded that the top 1% of American households owned 35.4% of the wealth and the top 10% owned 77% of the wealth while the bottom 80% owned just 11%. The same study also showed the top 20% earn 59.1% of the national income. The Economic Pol-icy Institute reported in 2012 that the wealthiest 1% of

American households are on average 288 times richer than the median American household. The wealthiest man in America, Bill Gates, has more wealth than the bottom 45% of American households combined.

This concentration of wealth has occurred because the government has favored some businesses to the exclusion of others. This is an unsustainable model, as proven by history.

Socialism is a theory or system of social organization that advocates the vesting of the ownership and control of the means of production and distribution—capital, land, etc. in the community as a whole. In theory, public or communal ownership applies especially to natural resources and to large enterprises that require community cooperation.

Socialists believe that community ownership is an answer to poverty, great inequalities of wealth, and social unrest. They consider the establishment of any kind of private property as a theft from the community and that the sharing of property creates social harmony and progress, in contrast to the perceived competition and conflict generated by private property and capitalism.

Socialist theory was a large result of the revolutionary transformation of society during the industrial revolution. With the movement from the self-sufficient rural areas to the mushrooming urban factory areas, the workers were made dependent on the sale of their labor services for survival, since they no longer owned the means of production. Labor power then became a commodity to be bought and sold like any other commodity.

Karl Marx, the most influential socialist ideologist, viewed this as exploitation of the working masses. Marx viewed capital as a "social power" in addition to its usual technical definition and believed that economic discrepancies were morally reprehensible. The aim of socialism is to make all individuals equal on economic terms; to abolish the traditional class structure through the abolishment of all private property.

By democratic socialism, I mean a political system whereby socialism comes into being through democratic vote; the people vote it upon themselves, rather than it being imposed from the top by the government or a political dictatorship.

Beyond the seemingly nice theory, socialism has proven to be a miserable failure. What the theorists never seem to realize is that the only way to implement socialism is through government force. While they advocate cooperation, they in essence make cooperation obsolete by forcing it. Unless people are free to voluntarily choose cooperation and service, these concepts are entirely meaningless.

Socialism cannot work; it is wrong both in theory and in practice. The implementation of socialism requires the use of force at the expense of liberty, and it is highly inefficient in providing economic wants and necessities to the masses by replacing cooperative, enlightened self-interest with a central bureaucracy. It is at odds with human nature in its desire for economic equality because it effectively eliminates individual incentive to succeed. Under socialism it matters not whether you work hard or not; regardless of your efforts your will still receive the same compensation as that of everyone else.

Free enterprise is the ideal political economic arrangement. Many people make the mistake of confusing capitalism with free enterprise. While they are similar in ideology, the main differences are as regarding the ownership of property and the means of production and the role of government.

Under a true free enterprise system, the ratio of owners to laborers should be directly opposite of the ratio found under capitalism. Conceptually speaking, we can say that roughly 80% of the population would be owners of the means of production in free enterprise. The role of government under free enterprise would be strictly to protect inalienable rights and to treat all men and business entities equally before the law and nothing more, unlike capitalism wherein the government steps out of those bounds.

Speaking of a free market, in The Wealth of Nations Adam Smith wrote, "All systems either of preference or of restraint, therefore, being thus completely taken away, the obvious and simple system of natural liberty establishes itself of its own accord.

Every man, as long as he does not violate the laws of justice, is left perfectly free to pursue his own interest his own way and to bring both his industry and capital into competition with those of any other man or order of men."

Ludwig von Mises, an economist and staunch proponent of a free market, said, "Government . . . is the opposite of liberty . . . government is repression not freedom. Freedom is to be found only in the sphere in which government does not intervene. Liberty is always freedom from the government." Henry Hazlitt, also an economist, stated that, "Practically all government attempts to redistribute wealth and income tend to smother productive incentives and lead toward general impoverishment. It is the proper sphere of government to create and enforce a framework of law that prohibits force and fraud. But it must refrain from specific economic interventions. Government's main economic function is to encourage and preserve a free market."

Free enterprise means that a large majority of the population are owners of land, businesses, and capital; that an economy can regulate itself in a freely competitive market through the relationship of supply and demand, allowing cooperative self-interest to operate freely in the marketplace; that there is a minimum of governmental intervention and regulation; and that all men and business entities are treated equally before the law.

The Critical Conclusion

Now, what does all of this have to do with scarcity and abundance? Here's how it works: People who live in scarcity base their decisions off fear. They become selfish and feel victimized, they refuse to take responsibility for their lives, and they see entrepreneurs who profit as being exploitive. Because they use limited strategies based on scarcity, they don't experience real financial success from their own efforts. Their greatest desire is to feel secure.

All of these things add up to them voting for governments and political and economic structures which use the force of government to take care of them. They justify the government taking from one person or business to give to another. These are the types of people who vote themselves benefits from the national treasury.

From scarcity come all forms of forced, government-sponsored wealth distribution. By its very nature, scarcity leads to socialistic thinking. When people think that material things have intrinsic value, it also follows that all people should have equal things. To these types of people, equality refers to an equality of material goods. And since the free market leads to inequalities in material goods, and since they think that this is evidence of exploitation, they feel justified in engaging in what Frederic Bastiat called "legalized plunder" in his book The Law.

On the other hand, people who live in abundance have faith in principle, they choose to be responsible and transcend negative external circumstances, and they believe in personal productivity. They understand that profit is evidence of value creation. Because they succeed financially and otherwise, they have no need or desire for the government to give them benefits. They want the government to simply protect their rights, nothing more and nothing less.

The choice between scarcity and abundance determines every human action, every human desire, and every type of political and societal arrangement! That one critical choice determines the success or failure of mankind!

When we choose scarcity, ultimately it results in us choosing for others to take care of us. We end up with false security and no freedom. When we choose abundance, this ultimately results in responsibility, success, true security, and freedom.

Worst case Scenarios

On a personal finance level, the worst case scenario for those in scarcity seeking security is low net worth and low income. For those in abundance seeking freedom, the worst case scenario is for them to have collateralized assets with a low cash flow. In the realm of political economy, the worst type of security is outright slavery through dictatorship and communism.

However, the absolute worst case scenario on the side of freedom is capitalism with a class system.

Summary

Those that choose to believe in and live scarcity have the end goal to find security. On a personal level, their thoughts, actions, and strategies lead to net worth at best, and low net worth and low income at worst. On a political and economic level, these people use the force of government to achieve their end of security. They take from others to provide benefits for themselves. Ironically, the way they pursue security is precisely the thing that keeps them from ever finding it, because the only true security in life comes from living Soul Purpose, which can only happen in abundance.

Those that choose to believe in and live abundance have the objective to achieve personal and societal freedom. On a personal level, their thoughts, actions, and strategies lead to high portfolio income at best, and collateralized assets with low cash flow at worst. On a political and economic level, abundance leads to free enterprise. When abundance is mostly but not fully embraced, we end up with a class system and capitalism at worst. Those in abundance find and live their Soul Purpose, and ultimately, are the only ones who find both freedom and true security in life.

Here's how it looks on the Money Tree model featured on the following page:

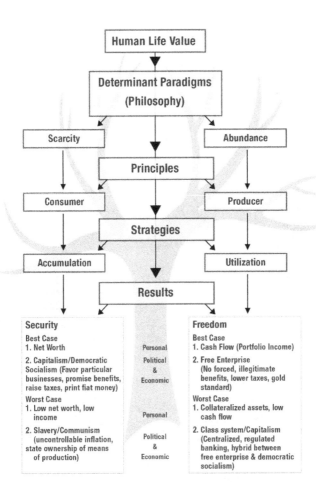

Chapter 7

Conclusion: The Big Picture

Scarcity creates fear and leads to the Consumer Condition. This leads to limited and risky investment strategies, which in turn result in nothing but net worth at best personally, and an entitlement mentality culturally. Abundance stimulates faith and leads to the Producer Paradigm. This leads to limitless and safe investment strategies, which in turn lead to high cash flow personally, and freedom culturally.

The purpose of this book is to help you see the tangible results of what happens when people choose scarcity and when they choose abundance, in order to help you consciously choose abundance. When people understand the real consequences of their thoughts, beliefs, habits, and actions, they are able to make better choices and experiences better results.

Furthermore, my intent has been to help you realize more fully that the root of your prosperity is you—not a product, not a strategy, not a government policy,

not a company benefit. Your human life value determines your level of success more than anything else.
Your human life value is increased by education, discipline, experience, and building relationships and is
decreased by ignorance, laziness, lack of experience,
and hurting relationships.

If you ever find yourself wondering what you
should invest in, the question is always, without exception, to invest in yourself and to increase your human
life value. The authors of this book have created many
powerful avenues for people to do so, which you can
read about in the next chapter.

After understanding the power of and developing
your human life value, the next step is to raise your
awareness of two determinant paradigms: scarcity
and abundance. This is such a critical choice because
everything you do in life is directly determined by how
you view the world.

If you view the world through eyes that see scarcity, it is inevitable that your decisions will be based
on fear, doubt, and worry; you will become selfish,
irresponsible, jealous, prideful, and suspicious; you
will fall prey to social myths; and ultimately live a limited life of regret.

If your view of the world is that of abundance,
your decisions will be based on faith, confidence, and
peace; you will cultivate self-assurance, humility, and
healthy critical thinking; you will be a responsible and
wise steward of all your resources; and be able to live
a life of greatness, contribution, and service.

The types of financial strategies that you use and how you use them are directly determined by your human life value, your paradigm, and your understanding of economic principles.

Accumulation strategies flow from a scarcity paradigm, they are based on dependence upon institutions, products, and other factors outside of the control of most people, they are made from a micro perspective of finances, they subject investors to multiple and considerable risks, and leave investors with very little control.

On the contrary, utilization strategies flow from abundance, they are based upon responsibility, they are made from a macro perspective of finances, they allow investors to mitigate their risk, and provide investors with much greater ability to determine financial results.

The results of scarcity are net worth on a personal level, and forms of government that use force to provide benefits and security to individuals, all at the expense of freedom. It is precisely because the root paradigm of scarcity that our nation suffers from an entitlement mentality today, or what we call the Consumer Condition. In contrast, the natural results of abundance and the Producer Paradigm are cash flow from portfolio income on a personal level, and forms of government that do nothing but protect equal rights and treat all individuals and institutions equally before the law. In short, scarcity leads to false security and a loss of freedom both personally and societally, while abundance is the root of any free society.

Here's how it looks on the Money Tree.

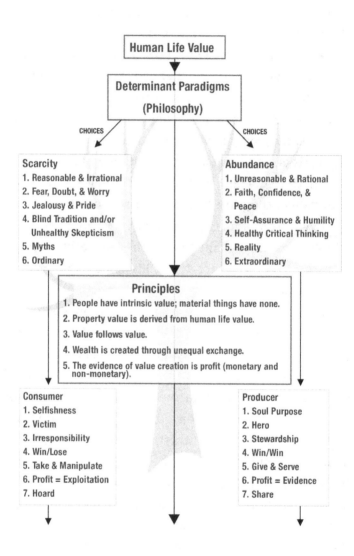

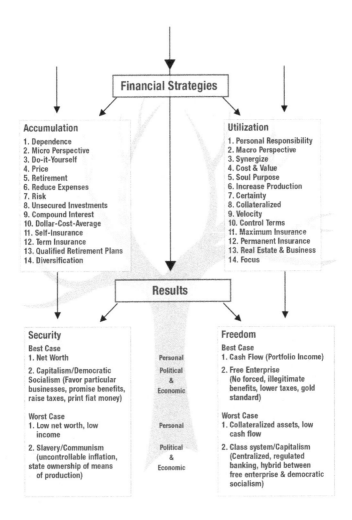

Financial Strategies

Accumulation
1. Dependence
2. Micro Perspective
3. Do-it-Yourself
4. Price
5. Retirement
6. Reduce Expenses
7. Risk
8. Unsecured Investments
9. Compound Interest
10. Dollar-Cost-Average
11. Self-Insurance
12. Term Insurance
13. Qualified Retirement Plans
14. Diversification

Utilization
1. Personal Responsibility
2. Macro Perspective
3. Synergize
4. Cost & Value
5. Soul Purpose
6. Increase Production
7. Certainty
8. Collateralized
9. Velocity
10. Control Terms
11. Maximum Insurance
12. Permanent Insurance
13. Real Estate & Business
14. Focus

Results

Security

Best Case
1. Net Worth

2. Capitalism/Democratic
Socialism (Favor particular
businesses, promise benefits,
raise taxes, print fiat money)

Worst Case
1. Low net worth, low
income

2. Slavery/Communism
(uncontrollable inflation,
state ownership of means
of production)

Personal

Political
&
Economic

Personal

Political
&
Economic

Freedom

Best Case
1. Cash Flow (Portfolio Income)

2. Free Enterprise
(No forced, illegitimate
benefits, lower taxes, gold
standard)

Worst Case
1. Collateralized assets, low
cash flow

2. Class system/Capitalism
(Centralized, regulated
banking, hybrid between
free enterprise & democratic
socialism)

Chapter 8

Action:
Where do we go from here?

To experience real, lasting results, you must take powerful and consistent action. Various tools and resources provided to help you take action and increase your Human life value.

As I stated at the beginning, there is simply no way that I can teach everything that I know about prosperity in one book. Although I have talked briefly about strategies, it's probably safe to say that you still have the question, "Okay, I get the whole abundance thing. Now what do I actually invest in?" If that's the case for you, I have one answer: invest in yourself and develop your human life value.

I have created numerous resources for you to do so and continue the education you have begun here. This book is a good introduction to the things I teach regularly, yet I also have programs where you can gain a depth of education about all of the concepts, principles, and strategies I have discussed in this book. The best place to start this education is through the Producer Power Hour mastermind, found at ProducerPowerHour.com.

The Producer Power Hour

Producer Power Hour (PPH) is a simple and effective system and support structure for creating favorable conditions for you to live the life of your dreams. In practical terms, The Producer Power Hour is, as the name suggests, a commitment of one hour a day towards becoming the most powerful version of YOU. The hour is started out with a platform of gratitude by using the first 10 minutes of the hour to express appreciation for your life in whatever way you'd like, such as prayer, meditation, affirmations, and/or journaling. The remaining 50 minutes consists of "ten minutes of transformation" in every major track of life, referred to as the five Tracks of human life value, which are the financial realm, the spiritual realm, the mental realm, the physical realm, and the social realm.

The Producer Power Hour is like your own daily mini "retreat". There is no greater investment that you could ever make than an investment in yourself. A major reason for why so many people are depressed and feel unfulfilled in this world is because their lives are not in harmony and balance. They may excel in some areas, but as they neglect other important components of a happy life, it eventually catches up to them.

For example, no amount of money can compensate for poor health, so getting rich by working long stressful hours and ignoring your physical body is a bad idea. But on the other hand, even those with perfect health will find it hard to enjoy life to the fullest without financial success and meaningful relationships, etc. There has to be a balance, because every aspect of our lives is intertwined. You cannot ignore one area and expect the rest to remain perfectly functioning. By the same token, improvements in one area can bring improvements to all.

Here are just a few of the benefits you can expect with the Producer Power Hour system:

A more purposeful, joyful and balanced lifestyle.

Empowering guidance and inspiration to help you become more aligned in every aspect of your life.

Greater access to the power that you already have within, with a larger capacity to express it.

Moments of inspiration and insight will become increasingly more frequent and powerful.

Self-Study

Anyone sincere about increasing their wealth and happiness is constantly educating themselves through reading, attending seminars, engaging with mentors, etc. Here is a list of books that we highly recommend as part of the process of self-improvement. You can also incorporate reading these books into your daily Producer Power Hour.

The Art of the Start by Guy Kawasaki

What Would the Rockefellers Do by Garrett Gunderson and
    Mike Isom

Killing Sacred Cows by Garrett Gunderson and Stephen Palmer

Autobiography of Benjamin Franklin

Basic Economics by Thomas Sowell

Before You Quit Your Job by Robert Kiyosaki

Cash Flow Quadrant by Robert Kiyosaki

The E-Myth Revisited by Michael Gerber

The Five Thousand Year Leap by Cleon Skousen

Portal to Genius by Garrett Gunderson and Leslie Householder

Jonathan Livingstone Seagull by Richard Bach

The Law by Frederic Bastiat

The Mainspring of Human Progress by H.G. Weaver

Positive Imaging by Norman Vincent Peale

The Power of Impossible Thinking by Wind, Crook, and Gunther

Rich Dad's Guide to Investing by Robert Kiyosaki

The Richest Man in Babylon by George S. Clason

The Richest Man Who Ever Lived by Steven K. Scott

Think & Grow Rich by Napoleon Hill

Thou Shall Prosper by Rabbi Daniel Lapin

True Prosperity by Yehuda Berg

Up From Slavery by Booker T. Washington

What is Seen & What is Not Seen by Frederic Bastiat

The Wisdom of Adam Smith edited by Haggarty & Rogge

The 8th Habit by Stephen R. Covey

The Power of Language

There is a direct relationship between our language and our paradigm; each affects the other, whether for good or bad. Since we know that our paradigm determines our results, we must find ways to influence and shape our paradigm for good. One powerful tool for achieving this is to deliberately and consistently focus on the words that we use and how we use them.

Language is so powerful because we have the ability to speak things into existence. Energy and action are created with language; we tend to believe and follow those who speak like they believe. Language allows us to define things to provide distinction, and people then become empowered through distinctions. In other words, the more clearly we can define things, the easier it is to understand them, and the easier it then becomes to take action on the basis of those definitions and distinctions. It's also easier to communicate with others and to help them to take action.

Here are three general rules to follow when it comes to deliberately utilizing your language to positively influence your paradigm:

1. Be specific. Generalities do not call forth action; specifics are a call to action. For example, it's the difference between saying, "I'd like to be financially free," and "I will be financially free within one year from today. By financially free, I mean that I will have a portfolio income of $10,000 per month, with monthly

expenses not exceeding $7,000 per month." The more specific you are with your language, the empowering will be your plan of action. Remember that "someday" is today.

2. Use language which implies choice and accountability. Refuse to use words and phrases that infer that something is impossible, or that you have no choice or control. These include such things as, "I can't," "I don't have time," "He made me do it," "I have to do this," etc. Replace these words with things like, "I haven't learned how to do this yet," "I will make time for important things," "I chose to do it based on his insistence," "I choose to do this etc." This one simple thing can create a fundamental shift in outlook for you. The first phrases imply that you have no or limited choice and accountability; by replacing them with words that imply choice and accountability, you will develop much greater ability to make wise and conscious choices.

3. Replace expectations with preferences. Expectations lead to attachment and expectations, which leads to disappointment and discouragement. Your task is to learn to do things because they are right, regardless of the consequence. This can be accomplished through carefully chosen language. Replace "I expect" with "I prefer."

All of us grow up with lies in our heads from social myths, and then we reinforce those lies every time we use language that implies that we have no choice with our actions, and that we are not accountable. These lies make our thought patterns lazy and routine; when we subconsciously believe that we "have" to do things then we automatically shut off our creative capability of thinking of other possibilities. Create your ideal life by being careful and deliberate about the language that you use.

The Financial Freedom Personal Declaration List

One of the best ways to get the process of prosperity going is to ask questions. Our brains are designed to answer the questions we ask. The more questions we ask, the more answers we receive.

Another crucial thing is that we ask the right questions. It deliberately creates discontentment in your current path. Discontentment provides the necessary awareness for anyone to take any action. Questions help you to dig deep into your mind and life to uncover areas of discontentment that may be hidden through habit and lack of consciousness. As you discover this discontentment, you are far more likely to take action and create real, lasting transformation in your life.

To help you with this process, I have created the following exercise which will help you to identify and give more meaning and understanding to your passions, interests, abilities, and desires. Please take your time to complete this exercise by answering the following questions in detail.

1a. If money was no object, what would you spend your time doing?

_____

_____

_____

_____

_____

1b. What would your life be all about?

_____

_____

_____

_____

_____

1c. What would you do day-to-day?

_____

_____

_____

_____

_____

1d. When will you start doing these things?

_____

_____

_____

_____

_____

1e. What is preventing you from doing these things now?

_____

_____

_____

_____

_____

1f. Are those the things you value most in life?

_____

_____

_____

_____

_____

2. Would you like to be free to spend your time and your money on the things that mean the most to you?   ☐ Yes   ☐ No

3. Are your actions consistent with your words?

_____

_____

_____

_____

_____

4. Who are you telling about what you want?

_____

_____

_____

_____

_____

5. Are you sure of what you want?   ☐ Yes   ☐ No

6. Does it matter what circumstances you encounter along the way?   ☐ Yes   ☐ No

7a. Who is accountable for your success or failure?

_____

_____

_____

_____

_____

7b. Is that regardless of circumstance?   ☐ Yes   ☐ No

7c. Do you want financial freedom only if you get lucky, or do you want it no matter what?

_____

_____

_____

_____

_____

8. What would need to happen to live your ideal life?

_____

_____

_____

_____

_____

9. Have you defined your conditions of satisfaction?

_____

_____

_____

_____

_____

10a. What action steps should you do immediately?

_____

_____

_____

_____

_____

10b. What things will you accomplish over the next 90 days? What are the critical action steps?

_____

_____

_____

_____

_____

10c. What do those things lead to over the next year? What will happen then?

_____

_____

_____

_____

_____

10d. What do you prefer your life to look like in three years? Five years?

_____

_____

_____

_____

_____

11. What is your major definite purpose in life?

_____

_____

_____

_____

_____

12. What is your vision of your best self and your best life?

_____

_____

_____

_____

_____

13a. Who have you enrolled in your vision? Who should you enroll?

_____

_____

_____

_____

_____

13b. When do you share your vision?

_____

_____

_____

_____

_____

13c. Can you accomplish this vision by yourself?   ☐ Yes   ☐ No

13d. What is the impact and cost to being small in your vision?

_____

_____

_____

_____

_____

13e. Are there things in your life today that take you away from your vision? Why?

_____

_____

_____

_____

_____

14. What legacy are you leaving?

_____

_____

_____

_____

_____

15. Would they make a Hollywood movie of your life?
☐ Yes   ☐ No

16. What do we hide by never failing?

_____

_____

_____

_____

_____

17. Who are you impacting?

_____

_____

_____

_____

_____

18a. If you were doing exactly what you wanted, what would that be?

_____

_____

_____

_____

_____

18b. Would you ever want to stop doing that?   ☐ Yes   ☐ No

19. What things do you value most in life?

_____

_____

_____

_____

_____

20. Is money important? ☐ Yes ☐ No

21. What is the root of money?

_____

_____

_____

_____

_____

22a. Can money impact your health?

_____

_____

_____

_____

_____

22b. Can relationships impact your health?

_____

_____

_____

_____

_____

22c. If so, what would you do with the extra time?

_____

_____

_____

_____

_____

23. What things can/should you eliminate from your life that are currently draining your energy?

_____

_____

_____

_____

_____

24. Does anyone else have more time than you?

_____

_____

_____

_____

_____

25. What can you do to provide more value in the world?

_____

_____

_____

_____

_____

26. Are your results evidence of what you say your priorities are?

_____
_____
_____
_____
_____

27. When are you going to be a cause in the matter of your life?

_____
_____
_____
_____
_____

28. Are you willing to give up who you are today to be who you could become?   ☐ Yes   ☐ No

29. What are you afraid of?

_____
_____
_____
_____
_____

30a. How can you eliminate that fear in your life?

_____
_____
_____
_____
_____

30b. What affect would eliminating fear have on your life?

_____

_____

_____

_____

_____

31a. How can you create more faith in your life?

_____

_____

_____

_____

_____

31b. What effect would that have?

_____

_____

_____

_____

_____

Summary

Taking action is the only way that you can fundamentally and consistently change your life for the better. In this chapter, I have provided several tools and resources to help you take action and continue the process of increasing your human life value and choosing abundance. These include joining the Producer Power Hour mastermind, continuous self-study, being conscious about and choosing your language deliberately, and completing the Financial Freedom Personal Declaration List.

There are three basic steps one must take to unlock success . . .

Step #1: MINDSET/PERSPECTIVE:

Your current results in life—your "fruit"—were created by your past beliefs, mindset & perspective. To create anything different in the future requires a different set of beliefs and a completely different way of seeing the world. As Robert Kiyosaki, author of the *New York Times* bestseller Rich Dad Poor Dad explains, "the difference between the poor, middle class and the rich is not that the rich think slightly different but that they think the complete opposite of the poor and middle class."

The Money Tree starts you down that road of thinking completely different. It will help you begin clearing some of the blocks that hold you back from experiencing economic freedom. To continue this process, we recommend going producerpowerhour.com to have daily tools and strategies to create an empowering mindset & perspective about money.

So now you have the first key, but is mindset alone enough?

NO!

A powerfully abundant Perspective and Mindset will get someone into the game of economic freedom and possibility, but it is far from the finish line.

Step #2: A PURPOSE & A PLAN
Purpose: Clarity of direction and a person's "WHY".
Plan: How that person is going to get there.

Once you have the right mindset, you'll want principled and practical advice on how to develop your own user-friendly blueprint or roadmap to get you to you desired outcome. Once you have your plan mapped out you'll have the second key, but does a full knowledge of what needs to be done guarantee success?

Is knowing what you should do enough?

NO!

Step #3: ACCOUNTABILITY—ACTION
The last element that must exist for one to produce the financial fruit and transformation that they are seeking for is the power of ACTION. All of the positive thinking in the world combined with a world-class plan is worth little without execution and action.

Think of it this way, do you think that the United States has the highest rate of obesity in the world because we lack information on how to be more physically active and eat healthier foods? Is it because people do not have the knowledge or desire to be fit and healthy?

NO!

We have more information at our fingertips than any generation of Americans have ever had before, yet we struggle more with our health physically and financially than ever before.

Why?

Accountable Action . . . we all need accountability, which includes teams and partners who hold us accountable in taking the specific actions upon which success is guaranteed. Otherwise, it's just too easy to put off change, and stay permanently stuck in the same ruts.

The Solution Producer Power Hour

BONUS: For lasting impact and sustainable change please visit ProducerPowerHour.com. Without the support of like-minded, abundant individuals, the world brings daily challenges that can oppose wealth and abundance. Through the proper network, ongoing resources, and accountability the probability of success skyrockets. In times of chaos, it is essential to have a group to support you. You are not alone and growth is not a do-it-yourself game. The hardest part is finding people of the same ilk and vision. We have done the heavy lifting for you.

So, in addition to the book, visit www.producer-powerhour.com tap into the group, resources, and content. Your free trial into the mastermind is at your fingertips. Click the "Join Today" button to get started!

9 781722 501228